Acknowledgments

Science and Plants for Schools and the Field Studies Council are grateful for permission to include the following copyright material:

Photographs. John Bebbington – figures 3(b), 12 (inset); Leighton Dann – figures 6, 7, 8; Maggie Bolt – figures 10(a), (b).

Artwork. All artwork, including cartoons, is by Anne Bebbington, with the exception of Linda Gray – figures 1, 3(a).

Cover artwork. Anne Bebbington.

Members of the Writing Group: Anne Bebbington (FSC), Colin Bielby (Manchester Metropolitan University), Janette Kean (Learning and Teaching Scotland), Ruth Thomas (Cavendish School) and Erica Clark (SAPS, editor).

Contents

Introduction

This series of activities aims to cover work that must be undertaken with plants as part of the Primary Curriculum (e.g. in Key Stages 1 and 2 in England, Wales and Northern Ireland, Scottish Primary P1 to P7 or equivalent). The activities have been developed by SAPS in collaboration with FSC (Field Studies Council).

The activities are being developed under a number of themes, each of which is published in a separate booklet and is also presented as website material (see SAPS website).

- **The parts of a plant and their functions.**
- **Reproduction and life cycles – the flower, fruits and seeds.**
- **Living processes and what plants need to grow.**
- **Grouping and classification.**
- **Plants in their natural environment.**

Within each set of topics, you will find different types of activities. Some are based in the classroom while others involve growing plants outside (say in tubs in a school yard or in a school garden) or making observations of plants growing in the wider environment. Teachers are encouraged to let pupils explore links between classroom and outdoor fieldwork activities.

The activities give emphasis to the growing of plants so that pupils can make first-hand observations, often on their own plant, and become familiar with plants and how they grow. This is supported by a range of activities that let pupils explore how to make models of plants, card games that reinforce their learning and simple investigations that help them find out more about how plants work. You may not wish to use all the activities in a set, but you will find a good range to choose from, to suit your class and curriculum requirements.

Each topic includes a description of the activity and appropriate information for teachers. There may also be 'pupil worksheets', particularly with the activities intended for older pupils. An important feature in this series is the inclusion of 'Background information for teachers', written to give advice and guidance to teachers less familiar with botanical jargon or who lack confidence in their teaching on plant topics. In some cases, these notes indicate further sources of information that may be helpful to teachers. These links may be to other publications and to useful websites.

The illustrations have usually been drawn from living plant material, so they are fresh, botanically accurate and realistically show what a pupil is likely to see. The activities are also generously supported by photographs - again many taken specially for this series.

At the end of each activity, you will find a 'Curriculum Links' box, to help you see where you could use this activity within the appropriate national curriculum framework.

Parts of a plant and their functions is the first booklet (theme) in the series. This topic introduces pupils to the basic parts of a flowering plant – the root, stem, leaf and flower. It provides a range of activities that include growing plants from seed (inside or outside the classroom), ways of making simple models of a plant and card games that are fun but at the same time reinforce pupil learning and help them to be ready to move on to the next stage.

Remember you can use Curriculum Links (on the SAPS website) to find more material to give support within your teaching programme.

Parts of a plant
➲ *Teacher Guidance*

Growing seedlings
Activity 1: Growing seedlings in the classroom (1)

Resources

☐ *Film pots (film cans) with wick (e.g. from capillary matting or J-cloth)*

☐ *Seed compost*

☐ *Small bag of vermiculite*

☐ *Packet of seeds, e.g. mustard (or see Further activities 3)*

☐ *Water*

☐ *Magnifying glasses (optional)*

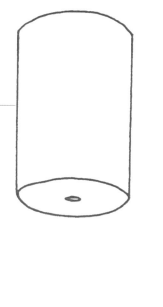

Preparation for the activity

• Collect sufficient film pots for your class. (You should allow enough for one film pot for each child, even though they may work in pairs or groups of three or more.) Translucent or black film pots can be used. (See *Student Sheet 9 on the SAPS website.*)

• Mix an equal amount of seed compost and vermiculite, breaking up any lumps in the compost. Vermiculite is available in garden centres. It helps keep the soil mixture moist, preventing drying out but you can manage without it.

• With younger children, you may prefer to moisten the soil and add it to the pot yourself before the lesson (*see below*).

The activity

Figure 1. Preparing your film pot. Make a hole in the base of a film pot and insert a wick. **(see Student Sheet 9 on the SAPS website.)**

Week 1

• Add approximately 1 teaspoon of soil and approximately 1 teaspoon of water to each pot. (That is about 5 cm³ / 5 ml or 1 plastic pipette full.) The soil needs to be just moist. If it is too wet, some seeds may rot.

• Drop three mustard seeds into the pot. Ideally you should drop one at a time so that they do not clump together.

• Place the pots in a light, warm position. Don't put them too near a radiator as excessive heat may kill the young seedlings. You may wish to keep them watered by placing the pot on capillary matting on a reservoir (see *Student Sheet 9*). (The children can also water their own pot by adding a few drops of water direct into the film pot if required.) If you have access to a light bank it would be ideal to put the pots under the light bank.

• After one week, or a minimum of five days (in a warm room), the seedlings should have developed enough for the children to see the main parts of the plant.

Week 2

• Now let the children look closely at the seedlings. Ask them to describe and discuss what they can see. *You can see the root hairs clearly. Children often describe these as being 'furry' but may associate them with the soil having gone 'mouldy' rather than realising the root hairs are part of the root.*

• Let the children gently pull the seedlings out of the pot. Some soil inevitably clings to the roots. This provides a good opportunity to discuss how the roots hold the plant in the soil.

• You can place the seedlings on black sugar paper and let the children use magnifying glasses to look at them. This gives the children an excellent opportunity to develop their observation skills. Parts of the plant can be seen really clearly this way.

NB. Beware of the pots drying out, particularly over a weekend or on a hot day.

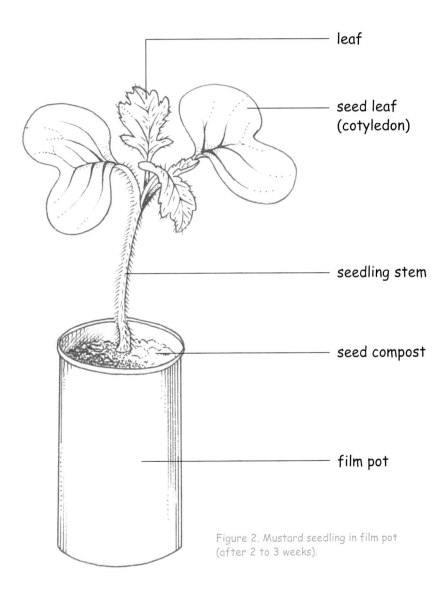

Figure 2. Mustard seedling in film pot (after 2 to 3 weeks).

FSC
BRINGING
ENVIRONMENTAL
UNDERSTANDING TO ALL

Further activities

1. Let the children draw their own seedling (see seedling diagram on page 7).

2. Play *Plant part dominoes* (see *Card Games* on page 11).

3. Grow different seeds so children can see the same pattern and different types of germination. Choose seeds like radish, tomatoes, mung bean, sunflower, pansy, French marigold (*Tagetes*).

4. Find some weed seedlings and allow children to try to pull up a few of them. They can see that the root anchors the plant (sometimes very firmly). Let them compare these weed seedlings with parts of plants in the classroom.

NB. Children should be discouraged from indiscriminately pulling up wild flowers. (See Scottish curriculum and the section called 'developing informed attitudes'.)

5. Ideas for reading (suitable for KS1 and Scottish curriculum level B).

The Enormous Turnip, by Ronne Randall and Emma Dodd (2003). Ladybird First Fairy Tales. This is a well known traditional fairy/folk tale for young children, about the difficulty of pulling a turnip from the ground and how more and more people join in to help pull it out. It demonstrates the strength of the root.

Rosie Plants a Radish, by Petty and Alex Scheffer (1998). Macmillan's Children's Books. This tells the story of Rosie, a rabbit who loves radishes. Children can read about how she plants her radish seeds, watches the plants grow and finally pulls up the radishes. They can see what is actually happening to the plant under the ground.

Jasper's Beanstalk, by Nick Butterworth and Mick Inkpen (1993). Hodder's Children's Books. Cat finds a bean and decides to grow a beanstalk. Each day cat does something different to encourage growth, but what he does not give it is time!

The Tiny Seed, by Eric Carle (1997). Puffin Books. Another book that helps demonstrate germination.

Curriculum links

National Curriculum (Sc2)	**KS1: 3b, 3c; KS2: 3c**
QCA guidelines – Scheme of work	**Unit 1B; Unit 2B; Unit 3B**
Scottish ISE 5-14 framework/attainment targets	**LT-B2.3, LT-B2.4**

Growing seedlings

Activity 2: Growing seedlings in the classroom (2)

Resources

☐ *1.5 litre plastic mineral water bottle (the flat-sided ridged bottles are particularly good for this activity)*

☐ *Petri dishes (9 cm diameter)*

☐ *Filter paper, 9 cm diameter (or discs made of any strong absorbent paper, using the lid of a petri dish as a template)*

☐ *Packet of seeds, e.g. mustard (or see Further activities 1)*

☐ *Water*

☐ *Permanent marker pen (fine)*

Preparation for the activity

• Cut a 1.5 litre plastic bottle as shown in diagram to form a boat shape. (If you have a round bottle, you may need to stabilise it, for example with blu-tak or plasticine.) (See *Student Sheet 5 on the SAPS website.*)

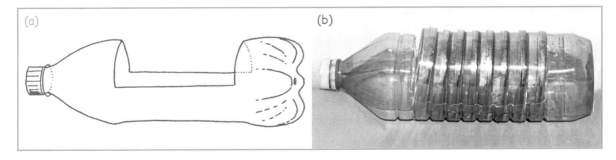

Figure 3. Plastic bottle (a) cut and ready to hold petri dishes (b) holding petri dishes.

• Place the filter paper discs in the lids and wet thoroughly. Pour off excess water and make sure there are no air bubbles under the paper disc. If using absorbent paper draw around the lid of the petri dish then cut out discs of the paper to fit the lid of the petri dish.

• Pour water into plastic bottle boat to depth of approximately 2 cm.

• With a fine permanent marker pen, draw a line across the inside of the lid of the petri dish about one-third from the top. Write numbers 1 to 4 along the line, about 1 cm apart.

Note that each bottle can hold up to 10 petri dishes. Each petri dish is suitable for growing up to four seeds.

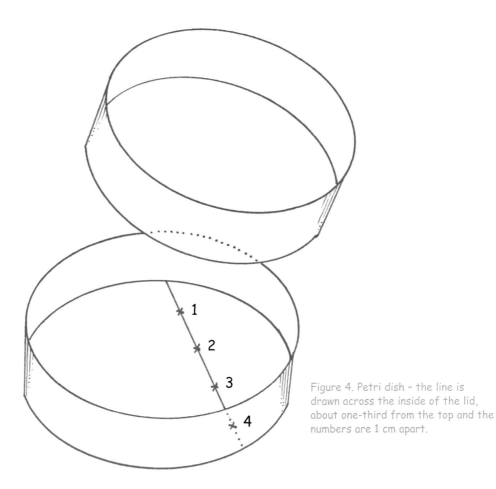

Figure 4. Petri dish – the line is drawn across the inside of the lid, about one-third from the top and the numbers are 1 cm apart.

The activity

- Put the lid of the petri dish, with its wet paper disc, flat on the table.

- Give each child a petri dish and let them place up to four seeds close to a number along the line.

- Put the bottom of the petri dish on top of the lid and label it. Leave the dish flat on the table for at least 10 minutes. (This gives the seed time to produce a secretion that helps the seed stick to the paper disc.)

- Gently pick up the dish and place it on its side vertically in the bottle boat. The bottom of the paper disc should be in the reservoir of water. *Any seeds that fall in the water will not germinate and grow successfully. You may replace these if you wish.*

- Place the boat bottle with the petri dishes in a light, warm place in the classroom. Don't put them too near a radiator as excessive heat may kill the young seedlings. If you have access to a light bank it would be ideal to put them under the light bank.

- Over the following week children are able to observe the following:

  1. The seed swells and the seed coat splits (normally within 24 hours)

  2. The root emerges and grows (within 48 hours)

  3. Shoot and green seed leaves grow (by the end of the first week)

NB. If positioned in a too cold place these processes may occur more slowly or the seedlings may even die.

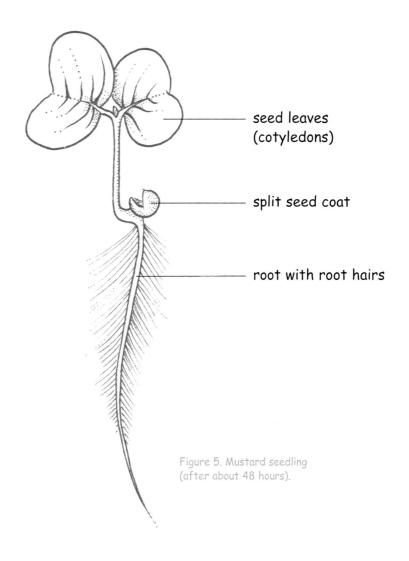

seed leaves
(cotyledons)

split seed coat

root with root hairs

Figure 5. Mustard seedling
(after about 48 hours).

Further activities

1. Grow other small seeds (like tomato, radish, pansy).

2. Find out which way roots and shoots grow (see *Primary OSMOSIS 22*).

Then see Further activities, listed under Growing seedlings in the classroom (1)

Curriculum links

National Curriculum (Sc2)	**KS1: 3b, 3c; KS2: 3c**
QCA guidelines – Scheme of work	**Unit 1B; Unit 2B; Unit 3B**
Scottish ISE 5-14 framework/attainment targets	**LT-B2.3, LT-B2.4**

FSC
BRINGING
ENVIRONMENTAL
UNDERSTANDING TO ALL

Parts of a plant
➡ *Teacher Guidance*

Growing a sugar snap pea

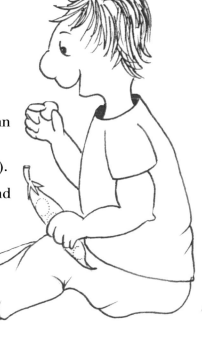

Plants commonly grown in schools include sunflowers and beans. As an alternative, we suggest a sugar snap pea for the following reasons:

- It is relatively hardy and can be planted early in the year (February or March).

- It has a short life cycle and will flower within 12 weeks (June) and produce peas by the end of the summer term (July).

- The peas produced are safe and enjoyable for pupils to eat (even when raw).

Resources

Outside

- [ ] *Tub (e.g. wooden or plastic)*
- [ ] *Potting compost (or garden soil)*
- [ ] *Netting for support (wire or plastic)*
- [ ] *Twigs, sticks, bamboo canes or string (for support)*
- [ ] *Sugar snap pea seeds*

Inside *(into pots)*

- [ ] *Flower pots (e.g. 16 cm diameter)*
- [ ] *Growing medium / potting compost*
- [ ] *Stakes (e.g. wooden kebab sticks)*
- [ ] *Sugar snap pea seeds*

Planting

1. *Directly into a garden area or tub*

- Sow the seeds straight into a small garden area or tub, outside, in February or March.

- Follow the instructions on the seed packet.

- If possible, prepare the garden area beforehand by digging in some garden compost.

2. *In small pots in the classroom*

Alternatively, peas can be started in small pots in the classroom, then planted outside later.

- Use any planting system you are familiar with – or try the SAPS planting system for radishes (see *Student Sheet 9 on the SAPS website*).

- Avoid over-watering or drying out – these are common problems when growing plants in the classroom. The SAPS system helps prevent these problems.

- Before transplanting into the garden or tubs, you need to 'harden off' these seedlings by placing them outside during the daytime for about a week. (This lets them get used to the colder conditions outside.)

Figure 6.
Sugar snap pea plant.

In a trial run, we sowed some sugar snap peas in a large flower pot (approx. 20 cm diameter), using a mixture of potting compost with some vermiculite. We placed the pot in a plastic tray with water to maintain its water supply. We kept it under a light bank at a normal room temperature. Seeds sown on 20 March had emerged by 26 March and there were several healthy pea pods on 1 May. Very little maintenance was needed.

Figure 7.
Pea flower with tendril.

Figure 8.
Mature pea pod.

Care

• Seedlings need normal garden management, including weeding.

• Water the seedlings and growing pea plants in dry weather.

• Most varieties need support. You can push a few branched twigs into the ground beside the growing peas or make them into a tent for the pea plants to scramble over. Alternatively you can support them with strings or with wire netting or plastic netting.

Further activities

This activity can provide plenty of opportunities for cross-curricular links, or links to other science topics. See *SAPS website for more information*.

Curriculum links

National Curriculum (Sc2)	**KS1: 3b, 3c; KS2: 3d**
QCA guidelines – Scheme of work	**Unit 1B; Unit 2B**
Scottish ISE 5-14 framework/attainment targets	**LT-B2.3, LT-B2.4**

FSC
BRINGING
ENVIRONMENTAL
UNDERSTANDING TO ALL

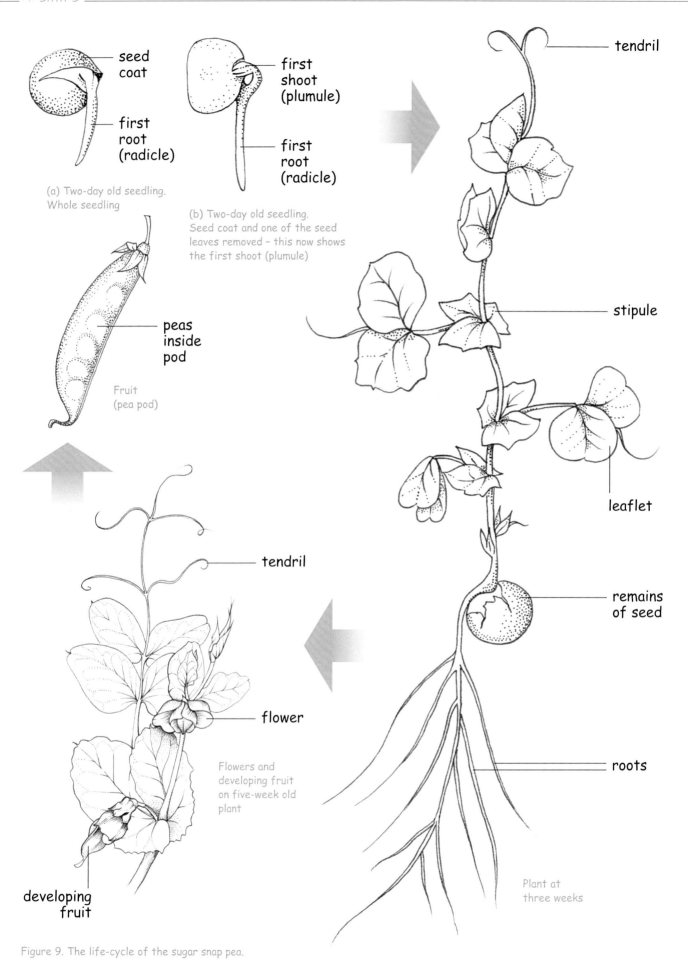

seed coat

first root (radicle)

(a) Two-day old seedling. Whole seedling

first shoot (plumule)

first root (radicle)

(b) Two-day old seedling. Seed coat and one of the seed leaves removed – this now shows the first shoot (plumule)

tendril

stipule

leaflet

remains of seed

roots

Plant at three weeks

peas inside pod

Fruit (pea pod)

tendril

flower

Flowers and developing fruit on five-week old plant

developing fruit

Figure 9. The life-cycle of the sugar snap pea.

For further information about structure of the pea leaf (stipule, leaflet, tendril), see *Background information for teachers*.

Parts of a plant
➡ *Teacher Guidance*

Games with cards

These are useful activities for 'starters', 'plenaries' and identifying children's misconceptions. Sets of cards are available as templates for you to photocopy (see templates for *Card Sets* on pages 22 to 25). Alternatively you can download them from the **SAPS** website. You can then make up sets of cards for your class.

Activity 1: Flash cards

Use card set 1. On these cards, the name is correct for the picture. The teacher shows the picture and the child reads the name.

Activity 2: Loop cards (plant part dominoes)

Use card set 2. These cards have names on the left but the picture on the right does not correspond with the name. The design of the cards is such that you can start with any picture and match it with the correct name on another card, so that all cards form a loop. Below we give a range of ways that these cards can be used to reinforce the names of the parts and encourage the children to read the terms.

1. **Whole class activity.** The teacher displays the four cards on a board. You can read the plant part name on a card and children choose correct picture on another card. Then read the name on that second card for children to identify the next picture on a third card and continue until all four cards are matched and in a loop.

2. **Whole class activity.** Divide the class into four groups. Each group has one of the four cards. One group reads out the name on its card and the group with the corresponding picture identifies itself. They then read out the name opposite their picture and another group then identifies itself and so on.

3. **Small group activity.** Divide the class into groups of four (or pairs of two). Each group has one set of the four cards shared out. One reads out the name on its card and the child with the corresponding picture identifies himself/herself. He/she then reads out the name opposite their picture and another child with the correct picture continues the game.

Modifications to any game. Get all the class to stand at the start, then once the child has read out a card he/she can sit down. You can time the loop game and then repeat to improve their speed of response.

Activity 3: Snap

Use card set 1. Prepare the cards by cutting them up so that you separate the names from the pictures. You need four sets for each group of children. Divide the class into small groups. Each group has 32 cards and plays the traditional game of 'Snap'.

Modifications to the game. Match names with names; match pictures with pictures; match names with pictures.

Activity 4: Memory game of matching pairs

Use card set 1. Prepare the cards by cutting them up (separating names from pictures as in activity 3). You need two sets for each pair of children. Each pair has eight cards and plays the traditional game of placing the cards face down then, in turn, tries to select two cards that match, either in name or by the picture. A more advanced game would be to match a name with the correct picture.

Activity 5: Happy families

Use card set 1. Prepare cards by cutting them up (separating names from pictures as in activity 3). You need four sets for each group of children. Divide the class into groups of four. Each group has 32 cards and plays the traditional game of 'Happy families'. The first child to collect a complete set of four names and four pictures is the winner.

Activity 6: Traditional game of bingo

Use the template Bingo card (see *page 26*). Fill in the three blank spaces with either the words or pictures from 'Parts of the plant'. You can cut out the words or pictures from card set 1.

Here are some examples of bingo cards you could prepare. Each group will need a different bingo card.

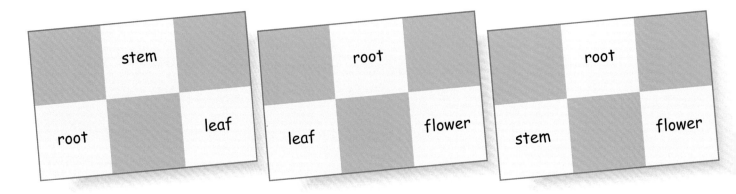

The teacher calls out the name or shows a picture of the plant part. The child covers over the corresponding word / picture until all three words / pictures have been covered. This is best played in small groups because of the high success rate.

Alternatively, give the children a blank bingo card and get them to choose their own three words (from root, stem, leaf, flower) and write them in any order in the blank spaces. They can copy the words from the board and this will encourage them to write out these key words.

Activity 7: Plant splat

Use the splat parts of a plant grid. Two versions of the grid are provided and you can adapt them further for your own use. You can, for example, replace the words with pictures to represent the four parts (root, stem, leaf and flower).

You can use the grids to make overhead transparencies (OHTs) and then use an overhead projector to project them onto a wall. Alternatively, you can download an electronic copy from the SAPS website and project this onto a wall from a laptop connected to a data projector or you can use an active white board.

The projected image needs to be at an appropriate height and size so that children can place their hands over each of the words in the grid. Alternatively, the children can use a 'prop' that will reach and cover each word. An idea for this would be a large two-dimensional flower shape, cut out of card and stuck to a short stick like a fly swatter.

Divide the class into two teams. One child from each team stands at the side of the grid projected onto the wall. The teacher asks a question and the first child to cover the correct square, shouting 'splat' at the same time, wins a point. Then repeat with another child, and so on.

A livelier version is to have several teams, each with a team leader. The team then discusses together before the team leader runs to the grid on the wall, covers the answer and shouts 'splat'.

Here are some questions you can use.

What is the name of the part of a plant...

...that is brightly coloured?

...that holds (anchors) it in the ground?

...where seeds are made?

...that is green and is joined to the stem?

...that is usually under the ground?

...that is usually tall and straight?

...that bees visit?

...that holds the flower high in the air?

Curriculum links

National Curriculum (Sc2)	**KS1: 3b**
QCA guidelines – Scheme of work	**Unit 1B**
Scottish ISE 5-14 framework/attainment targets	**LT-B2.4**

FSC

BRINGING
ENVIRONMENTAL
UNDERSTANDING TO ALL

Parts of a plant
➡ *Teacher Guidance*

Create a plant

Create a plant using a variety of materials from the box. The box can contain materials that could represent different parts of the plant. Depending on your selection, this can be used as a cross-curricular activity. You could, for example, use this as an opportunity to talk about sustainability and only put recycled items in the box. Let the children select from the box and construct a plant. They can stick it down on card. You can discuss with the children what each item represents as they construct the plant.

Here are some ideas for materials that you could use:

Part of plant	Possible materials
Stem	• hollow pipe insulating foam • card tubing from foil/cling film • drinking straws
Roots	• long 'art' pipe cleaners • string • wool
Flower	• coffee filter (can be coloured) • cake cases • cake doily • milk bottle tops • paper plates
Leaves	• card/paper

You will also need a set of labels for each part of the plant. These are provided as templates (page 29) for you to photocopy or you can download them from the SAPS website.

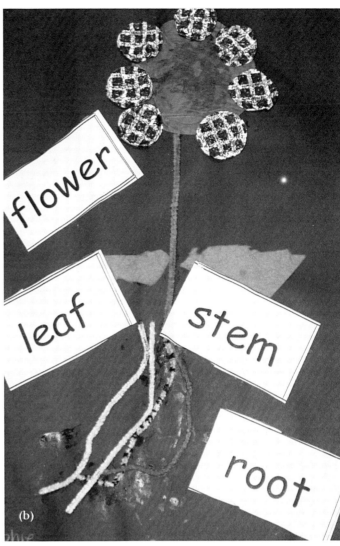

Figure 10. Some plants 'created' by children (at The Cavendish School).
(a) **flower** – *egg box and milk bottle tops;* **leaf** – *green card;* **stem** – *drinking straw;* **root** – *pipe cleaners.*
(b) **flower** – *tissue paper and milk bottle tops;* **leaf** – *green card;* **stem** – *pipe cleaner;* **root** – *pipe cleaners.*

Curriculum links

National Curriculum (Sc2)	**KS1: 3b**
QCA guidelines – Scheme of work	**Unit 1B**
Scottish ISE 5-14 framework/attainment targets	**LT-B2.4**

Parts of a plant
➡ *Teacher Guidance*

Building a plant game

Templates of the different parts of plants are provided in this booklet (pages 30 and 31) for you to photocopy and make your own sets for your class. (Alternatively you can download them from the SAPS website.) Use a different colour of card for each part. If you laminate the parts, they will last longer and you can use them again.

The children then use these parts to build a plant. Each group (or child) needs a board on which to assemble the plant.

If playing the game outside, each group (or child) has a container (say a tray, box or bucket) with four parts of the plant and the four labels of plant parts (root, stem, leaf, flower).

When told to 'start', the first child takes one piece (from the container), runs to the board, then places the part on the board and runs back to the container. The second child (or 'first child' again) takes a piece and runs to the board to find a suitable position to place the next part, then returns to the group. This is repeated until all the pieces and labels have been assembled on the board. All in the group then go to the board to check the plant and they can make any adjustments they think are needed. When satisfied it is correct, they all sit down. The first group to sit down beside a correct plant is the winner.

Alternatively, this can be used as a classroom activity, around a table. As a variation, they can be timed, and see who has assembled the flower most quickly, or how much they have done in a certain time (e.g. two minutes).

Curriculum links

National Curriculum (Sc2)	**KS1: 3b**
QCA guidelines – Scheme of work	**Unit 1B**
Scottish ISE 5-14 framework/attainment targets	**LT-B2.4**

Background information for teachers

These notes are provided to give teachers the background they may need when teaching these topics on plants. The vocabulary and words used are botanically correct. It is always advisable to keep closely to the standard terminology so that pupils have a firm foundation to build on and don't have to 'undo' their learning and vocabulary at a later stage. However, it is not intended that you pass these notes on to pupils in the form presented here.

Parts of a plant

At primary level, when learning about parts of a flowering plant, the children are first expected to recognise and name the root, stem, leaf and flower. These notes give you some extra information about these structures.

Root

The roots anchor or hold the plant in the soil. They take up water and dissolved mineral salts. [See *'Food' in plants*, page 20.]

Stem

The stem holds the leaves and flowers above the ground in their most appropriate position (for example, holding the leaves in the best position to get maximum light). The stem also contains vascular tissue (the transport system of the plant). Mineral salts and water are transported from the roots to the leaves and other parts of the plant. Sugars and other substances are carried away from the leaves.

Leaf

The main part of the leaf is the leaf blade and this is often joined to the stem by a stalk. The transport system in the stem continues through the stalk into the veins of the leaf. An important function of the leaf is to carry out photosynthesis.

Leaves at the base of the plant (known as basal leaves) are often different in shape and/or size from leaves higher up the stem (stem leaves).

At the base of the leaf stalk, there may be a pair of leafy outgrowths called stipules. You can see this on the diagram of the sugar snap pea. In some plants (such as the sugar snap pea), the leaves are deeply divided into separate leaflets. A leaf differs from a leaflet by having a bud at the point where it joins the stem. In the sugar snap pea you can also see that some of the leaflets are modified to form tendrils. If the first formed pair of leaves look different from other leaves they are probably seed leaves. These were part of the seed and provided a store of food for the germinating seed. The scientific name for a seed leaf is a cotyledon.

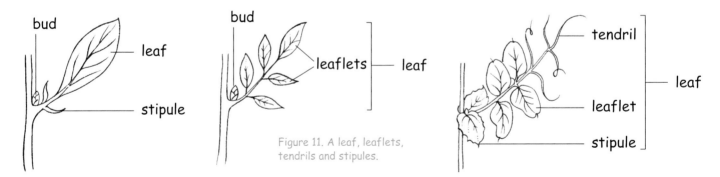

Figure 11. A leaf, leaflets, tendrils and stipules.

Bud

A bud is an immature shoot, sometimes consisting of immature flowers as well as leaves. The shoot is compressed and enclosed by protective scale leaves. All leaves have an axillary bud where the leaf stalk joins the stem. At the tip of the stem there will be a terminal bud.

Flower

The flower is the part of the plant where the seeds are made. [*For more information see the SAPS website.*]

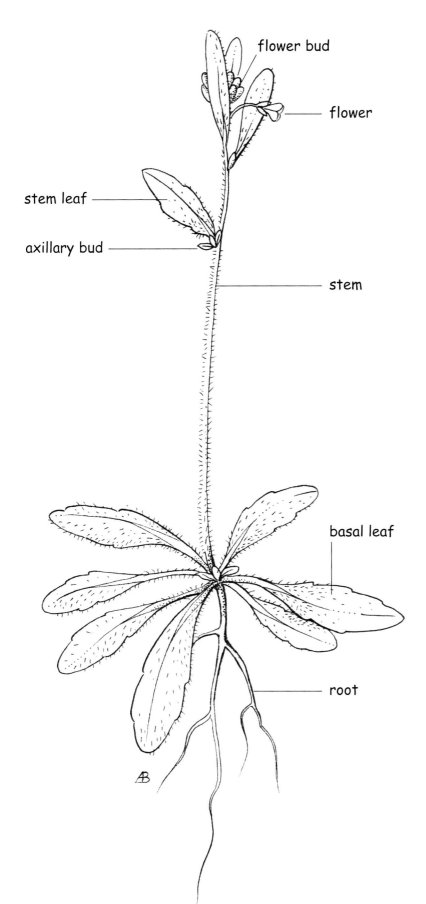

flower bud

flower

stem leaf

axillary bud

stem

basal leaf

root

Figure 12.
Thale Cress
(*Arabidopsis thaliana*).

General note

'Food' in plants

Food provides a source of energy for living processes.

Animals are known as consumers and obtain their energy from the plants and animals that they consume.

Green plants are known as producers and are able to trap energy from the sun, using the green pigment chlorophyll. This energy is used to produce sugars, by the process of photosynthesis. The sugars are subsequently broken down to provide the source of energy for living processes in the plants. Plants are therefore said to make their own food.

In addition to obtaining energy, all animals and plants need other substances to build up their cells and grow successfully. These substances include mineral salts. Animals obtain their minerals from the plants and animals that they consume. Plants usually obtain their minerals from water taken up by the roots, and this water contains dissolved mineral salts.

Children are often confused by use of the term 'food' particularly when they know that 'plant food' can be purchased (say from a garden centre) and added to the soil to 'feed' plants. (This is mainly mineral salts.) They should understand that in science, we link 'food' primarily with it being a source of energy.

Curriculum links

Parts of a plant

National Curriculum (Sc2)	**KS1: 3b, 3c; KS2: 3b, 3c**
QCA guidelines – Scheme of work	**Unit 1B; Unit 2B**
Scottish ISE 5-14 framework/attainment targets	**LT-B2.3, LT-B2.4, LT-C2.4**

Food in plants

National Curriculum (Sc2)	**KS1: 3b, 3c; KS2: 3b 3c**
QCA guidelines – Scheme of work	**Unit 1B; Unit 3B**
Scottish ISE 5-14 framework/attainment targets	**LT-B2.3, LT-B2.4**

Templates – for card sets, grids (bingo and splat) and plant parts

The templates given here (pages 22 to 31), are provided for you to make your own sets of cards, grids and plant parts. In this booklet they are available for you to photocopy. They are also provided on the SAPS website as both pdf and Word files. You can download the pdf files and use them as they are or you may prefer to adapt the Word files to your particular version of the card game.

It would be appropriate to make your card sets (pages 22 to 25) out of lightweight card and in some cases you may wish to use coloured card, though this is probably unsuitable for the sets with coloured parts of the flower. Alternatively, you can make good and durable sets by printing onto paper (or card), then laminating your pages. When you have your whole page, you then cut out the cards for use with your class.

Grids to use for bingo and splat are provided as templates on pages 26 and 27. Templates for plant parts are on pages 30 and 31.

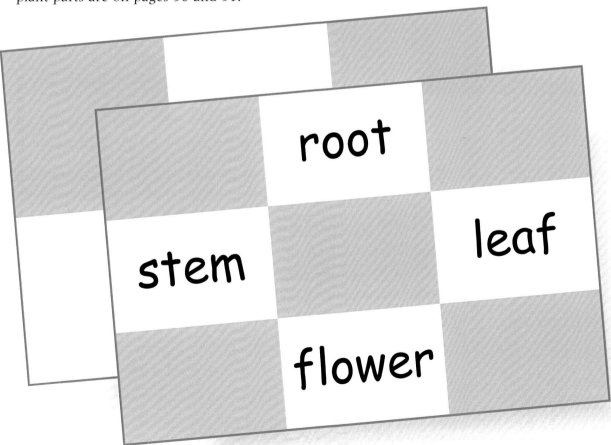

FSC
BRINGING
ENVIRONMENTAL
UNDERSTANDING TO ALL

Card set 1 *(use for activities 1, 3, 4, 5, 6)*

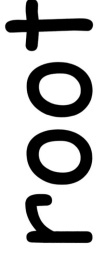

root

stem

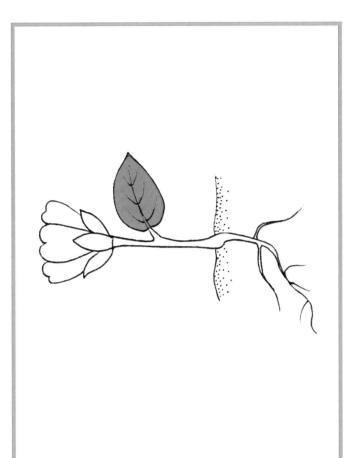

leaf

flower

FSC

BRINGING
ENVIRONMENTAL
UNDERSTANDING TO ALL

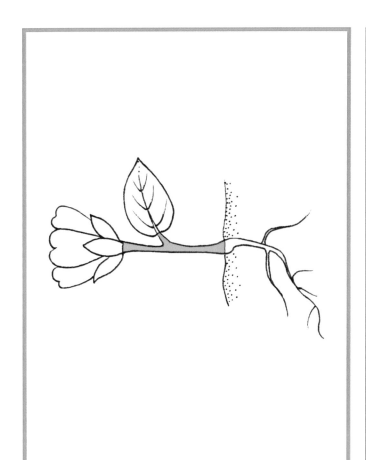

root

stem

FSC
BRINGING
ENVIRONMENTAL
UNDERSTANDING TO ALL

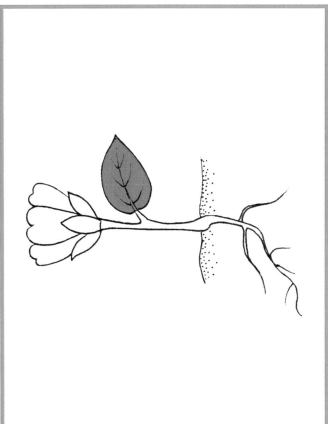

leaf

flower

FSC
BRINGING
ENVIRONMENTAL
UNDERSTANDING TO ALL

Bingo cards *(use for activity 6) to be adapted by teacher*

Parts of a plant and their functions

leaf

root

flower

stem

FSC

BRINGING
ENVIRONMENTAL
UNDERSTANDING TO ALL

SPLAT Parts of a plant grid *(use for activity 7)*

root

flower

leaf

stem

Create a plant *labels for parts of plant*

root	stem
leaf	flower

Build a plant game *templates 1*

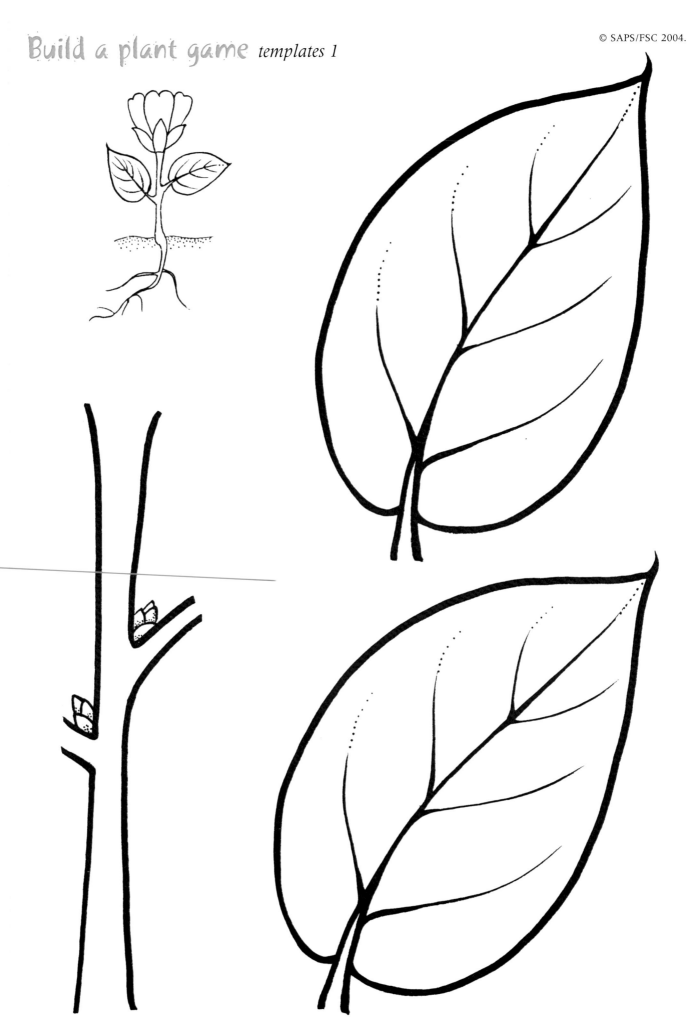

Notes

Notes

FSC

BRINGING
ENVIRONMENTAL
UNDERSTANDING TO ALL

FSC

BRINGING
ENVIRONMENTAL
UNDERSTANDING TO ALL

Notes

FSC

BRINGING
ENVIRONMENTAL
UNDERSTANDING TO ALL